BYGONE BOSHAM

BYGONE BOSHAM

by
ANGELA BROMLEY-MARTIN

PHILLIMORE

1978

Published by
PHILLIMORE & CO. LTD.,
Shopwyke Hall, Chichester, Sussex

© Text and illustrations Angela Bromley-Martin, 1978

ISBN 0 85033 310 5

Printed in Great Britain by
UNWIN BROTHERS LTD.,
at The Gresham Press, Old Woking, Surrey
and bound by
THE NEWDIGATE PRESS LTD.,
at Book House, Dorking, Surrey

CONTENTS

Introduction

Village Life

1. High Spring tide in the High Street
2. High water at Street End
3. The Quay completely submerged
4. George Martin
5. High Street opposite the 'Anchor'
6. Dolly Woods in the High Street
7. High Street during a Spring Tide
8. Fishermen's cottages
9. Schooners unloading by the Quay
10. Trading vessels lying alongside the Quay
11. Sailing Boats
12. Bosham Charter
13. One of the gravel barges
14. Carts belonging to A. H. Edwards
15. William Coward on a hay rick
16. Governess cart outside Church Farm
17. Church Farm House
18. Driving cows home for milking
19. Thatched barn at Church Farm
20. Edith Coward
21. George Brown, farmer and miller
22. Church and Quay meadow
23. Dairy at Mill House
24. Mill pond
25. The Brook
26. Cut Mill
27. Baker's cart outside the 'Gloucester'
28. Milk float
29. Chichester Dairies delivering at high tide
30. Mr. Norris the Carrier
31. Mr. Lemon the Carrier
32. Dustcart in Shore Road at high tide
33. Bosham Lane, leading to the sea
34. Bosham Lane during a high Spring tide

35. Bosham Lane at Chapel Corner
36. Mr. Redman the blacksmith and son
37. Outside the blacksmith's
38. Selwyn Lloyd with his dog
39. Selwyn Lloyd with his daughter
40. Young Selwyn Lloyd with Great Aunt Dora and mother
41. Young Selwyn Lloyd with his nurse
42. Mrs. Bryant, the cook at the Manor House
43. Two maids outside the Manor House
44. Duke the gardener at the Manor House
45. Mr. and Mrs. Pennett, housekeepers at the Manor House
46. Selwyn Lloyd by a governess cart
47. Dora Lloyd
48. Selwyn Lloyd with his wife and son
49. The Grange in 1913
50. Chapel Corner
51. Strange Hall
52. Broadbridge House
53. The keeper at the Tollgate
54. Duck shooters
55. Horse punted in a boat
56. Wilfred and Percy Gardener
57. View across the Creek
58. Brigham Arnold with his bride
59. The Village School
60. The Post Office
61. The Country Stores
62. The Walton Pub
63. Building the War Memorial
64. The completion of the War Memorial
65. The builders of the War Memorial
66. The procession for the unveiling of the Memorial
67. George Ede marching in the procession
68. The choir singing at the unveiling of the Memorial
69. Reverend Maunder unveiling the Memorial
70. A visit by the late Queen Mary
71. A visit by Queen Elizabeth
72. A visit by Queen Elizabeth
73. A map of 1825
74. Bosham village on 4 October, 1936

Churches

75. The Bayeaux Tapestry
76. Bosham Priory

77. Bosham Parsonage House
78. An engraving by Nibbs
79. An engraving showing the guard house
80. The Church in 1901
81. The Church in 1903
82. A sketch of the Church in 1911
83. The south aisle of the Church
84. The bell
85. The interior of the Church in about 1900
86. An etching of the crypt by Nibbs
87. George Arnold
88. A picnic party at Kingley Vale in 1914
89. The Congregational Church

Fishing and Shipbuilding

90. The quay in 1850
91. From the tower showing the oyster beds
92. The waterfront
93. Alan Arnold
94. An oyster boat
95. Phil Coombes and Charlie Stoveld
96. Charlie Stoveld
97. The 'Iona' with her crew
98. Arthur White
99. Ned Coombes
100. Lino cut of the 'Sugar Plum'
101. Fisherman scrubbing his boat
102. Bill and Jack Arnold
103. 'Thetis' alongside the Quay
104. The end of the Quay
105. Trading vessel alongside the Quay
106. Schooner at low tide
107. Schooner 'Nugget'
108. 'Emerald' being unloaded
109. Yacht 'May'
110. Selwyn Lloyd on a sailing trip
111. Stocking ship for the yachting season
112. Dinghies lined up at the Quay
113. Slipway of Apps' yard
114. Sketch of Apps' yard in 1888
115. 'Good Hope' nearly ready for launching
116. Thomas Apps
117. 'Good Hope' in full sail
118. Two small girls in front of the shipyard

119. Apps' in 1920
120. View of the village from near the school
121. 'Prince of Wales' motor vessel
122. 'Dolly Varden' being built at Smart's yard
123. Gregory Major with his parrot
124. Gregory Major mending nets
125. Mr. and Mrs. G. Major
126. Mr. and Mrs. Hickman
127. Edith Hickman as a child
128. Edith Hickman
129. 'Anchor' and the 'Ship' pubs

Fairs, Fetes and Regattas

130. Manor House decorated in 1902
131. Programme for the Swiss Fete in 1904
132. Maypole dancing at the Dutch Fete in 1907
133. Miss Heaver at the Dutch Fete
134. Selwyn Lloyd at the Dutch Fete
135. View of the Dutch Fete
136. Caroline Lloyd with her husband and son at the Dutch Fete
137. Selwyn Lloyd and 'Lanky' Williams at the Dutch Fete
138. Group of participants at the Dutch Fete
139. Old English Fete
140. Manor House party watching a regatta
141. Manor House party aboard 'Nellie'
142. Regatta of 1902 or 1903
143. Programme for the regatta of 1908
144. Regatta of 1910
145. Spectators in the m.v. 'Excel'
146. Greasy pole contest at the regatta of 1913
147. Sailing regatta in the 1920s
148. Poster for 1926
149. Fishing boats in the regatta
150. View of a regatta
151. Spectators shortly before the first World War
152. Committee boat
153. Admiral at a regatta
154. Chris Moore causing amusement
155. Pageant for the Jubilee of King George V in 1935 or the coronation of King George VI in 1937
156. Fair on Quay Meadow

INTRODUCTION

It was about 10 years ago that a local shipwright was helping my husband repair our boat. I asked Bert Merrett if he knew the story behind the term 'Men of Bosham', he being the grandson of one. In his reply he told me that I ought to go to see his old Mother, the late Lili Merrett, and thus started my interest in and collection of old photographs of Bosham.

I subsequently spent many happy hours with 80 year old Mrs. Merrett, looking through and copying from her vast pile of photographs and postcards as well as recording on tape all the stories she told me of her childhood and of what she remembered her parents and grandparents telling her. She also referred me to her friends and relations. Before very long I had a fund of photographs and information. My original plan was to get sufficient material to make a 16mm. 20 minute colour film of the history of Bosham, but long before that was finished, I had become addicted to collecting photographs, old postcards and books regarding the village of yester-year.

So, in the following pages, are some of the photographs gathered in the last 10 years. It will be a difficult task deciding which to put in and which to leave out. I hope that those I have chosen will prove to be of interest to many generations.

Bosham is unique. Decades ago there were many fishing villages along the Sussex Coast similar to Bosham but with the passing years, they have become towns or centres for caravan parks and holiday camps. I have often speculated as to why the tea rooms and fish bars have never been a part of the Bosham scene. Possibly it was the yachtsmen who, drawn to the village, purchased every available property. The possible café owners could not compete price-wise—and of course there were no sandy beaches near to draw the families and children. Today it would be extremely difficult to start any tea room or café as there are few places acceptable to the planning authorities, owing to the parking problem. Bosham is now a Conservation Area and this, along with the opposition from the local residents, would make any venture of this type well nigh impossible.

But Bosham has for a long time been one of the 'musts' for anyone touring around Sussex, one of its major attractions being its famous Church. The artists have come for at least two centuries for, in the British Museum, are two volumes of paintings of Sussex by Grimm in the period 1780-1795. Of his four paintings of Bosham there is one of the Church and Ecclesiastical College, one of the Vicarage and two of the Corbels and Pew Ends in the Church. Many engravings have been made from this artist's work. In the Southern Railway Guide to Stations of 1840, Bosham is stated as being a village popular with artists because of its beauty. Any visitor at that time would have had to walk one and a half miles from the station to the desirable painting spots along the shore—unless of course there was a horse drawn carriage available.

More recently Bosham has drawn the photographers and during my researches I have found half a dozen men who seemed to have covered Bosham fairly comprehensively with their cameras at the turn of the century. One of them was the local doctor who came out from Chichester daily in a gig and had his surgery in the house between the two pubs 'The Ship' and the 'Anchor Bleu' in the High Street. Dr. Buckle climbed the scaffolding placed around the Tower when it was being repaired in 1903 and produced two superb photographs of the surrounding area.

So today one sees a tidy, well-kept village, the old fishermen's cottages brightly painted, Quay Meadow green and open, the Quay itself in excellent order and the dinghies all in neat rows in the dinghy parks. But nowhere for a footsore tourist to get a cup of tea and a bun. This is all a very different picture to what the painters and photographers would have seen 50 or 100 years ago—but still as artistic as ever, in spite of the motley assortment of untidily parked cars, for the visitors to 'Happy Bosham'.

ACKNOWLEDGMENTS

There are so many people who have helped by lending photographs, that I find it difficult to name them all. I would like particularly to thank the following without whom this book would never have been possible:
Miss D. Lloyd, daughter of Hugh Selwyn Lloyd; The Misses E. and Mr. Coward of Bosham Stores; Mr. G. A. Osbon of the National Maritime Museum; Mrs. Efa Bevan (née Hickman); Mrs. Eva Purser (grand-daughter of Ernest Layzell, baker); Mrs. Anne Hector (née Dolly Woods); Mr. R. T. (Bogia) Combes; Mrs. E. Minster; Miss M. Stoveld; Mrs. A. Murray Brown; Mr. Leslie Holden; Mrs. I. Robertson; Mrs. (Sally) Trowill.

I would also like to thank Mrs. Valerie Lowdon for so cheerfully typing the text and captions many times as new pictures and more information came to light.

To all those, named and unnamed, who have helped in any way with the compilation of this book I would like to express my warmest thanks.

VILLAGE LIFE

Today we see in Bosham a village that has only existed in its present form for about forty years—that is a place for the tired and the retired, the weekenders and the yachtsmen. Prior to this new era, Bosham remained relatively unchanged for hundreds of years.

Twice a day the tide laps under the windows of the little cottages along the shore that were in former times occupied by the fishermen. Some fishermen had stone ramps alongside their homes up which they pulled their boats. Along the High Street and down Bosham Lane lived the shipbuilders and the families of the crews that sailed the Schooners which traded in and out of the Quay. These houses had to have high steps, both into their gardens and in front of their front doors, to keep out the sea water at the time of the very high spring tides twice a year.

There were also the farmers who grew the corn that fed the three or four mills in the area. The land around has produced some of the finest corn since Roman times. According to Domesday, a schedule of all land and property ordered by William of Normandy (the Conqueror) in 1086 for taxation purposes, there were 11 mills in operation at that time. Not all of these would have been actually in the village, but they were within the area. The Mill on the Quay was working until the 1930s and is now leased by the Lord of the Manor, Lord Iveagh, to the Bosham Sailing Club. The last miller also farmed the immediate area. He kept pigs on the meadow, while most of the village milk came from his cows that grazed the fields around the mill pond. Milk was delivered to front doors twice daily within a few hours of milking.

There were two or three bakers who also delivered bread to the front doors by donkey or horse cart—a four-pound loaf in 1900 cost 4¾d. At about ten o'clock on Sunday mornings, locals would be seen taking their joints along to the Bakehouses, or to an oven operated on Sundays only by the owner of 'The Ship' to be roasted in the bread ovens—it cost 2d. Few people had ovens of their own; they cooked on open range fires, the wood for which was gathered by the children from around the shore or in the woods. Enough wood floated in on the tides to keep the village well supplied.

Mains water did not reach Bosham until 1910. Before then water was obtained from the dip holes that were situated down Bosham Lane and fed from the moat of the Manor House—the moat going back to the time of Canute and Harold. Drinking water came direct from the Brook which runs beside the Church. The Brook is not a natural waterway, but may have been built as long ago as the Roman period. It leaves the natural water course three or four miles north of the village at Ratham Mill.

A butcher came down every Friday from West Ashling with a cartload of meat and set up shop in one of the oyster barns, next door to the 'Anchor'. Fisherwomen pushed their vendibles around the village on flat-topped barrows, calling out the prices as they went.

The children and their parents wore clothes passed down to them by previous generations. When new clothes were needed, there would be the excitement of a trip to Chichester, five miles away, in the Carrier's cart. The round trip cost 4d. There were those who worked in Chichester. They either walked—the footpaths are a shorter distance than the modern roads—or went by train, but the station was a good mile from the village and a ticket to Chichester cost 3d., a great deal of money in those days.

The roads were all dirt, becoming a dust bowl in dry weather and a quagmire in wet. In 1837, a new National School was built at the top of the creek, a few minutes' walk from the centre of the village. Only half the length of the High Path or Craut (a Saxon word meaning right of way) existed then, so a few hundred yards of the pathway was below high tide level. When this situation occurred the boys of the school had to fetch benches to form a footbridge, so all might arrive dryshod for school six days a week—they did get a half-holiday on Saturday.

1. High Spring tide up the High Street. On the left is the 'Anchor'. On the right is the oyster packing barn where in 1812 a breakaway group from the Parish Church held their first services under the direction of the Congregational Minister of Chichester. The butcher also held his 'shop' here on Fridays.

High Water, Bosham

2. High water at Street End when the water comes right up Bosham Lane. On the right is Folletts Grocery Shop, a building which has since been demolished together with the house.

3. The Quay completely submerged during a high Spring Tide in 1935. The sight of a car with water up to its floorboards is a common sight in Bosham around Shore Road, which is covered by water often twice a day. However, it is not often that the boats on the Quay are afloat.

4. George Martin, the brother of the owners of 'The Ship' and 'Anchor'. He owned many trading schooners which plied along the South Coast. He eloped in the 1870s, or 1880s with the daughter of the Vicar of Bosham, the Rev. Mitchell, and lived in the house called St. Martins in the High Street. Here he is with his daughter Nora (Pet) Martin and Thora, the daughter of his son, Glyn Martin.

5. The High Street opposite 'The Anchor' at the turn of the century. This area was mostly occupied by pigs, although when the fair came to Bosham once a year some of the stalls were placed around here.

6. Dolly Woods is the little girl walking along the High Street. Behind her is the 'Town Hall', which before the days of Rural District Councils was where the local authorities dispensed their duties. It was afterwards turned into five cottages. The shop beside Dorothy Woods is Folletts Grocery shop. On the right are the fishermen's cottages which bear such names as 'Bosham Castle' and 'Bosham Abbey'. The back of these houses face on to the sea.

7. The High Street during a high Spring Tide in 1935. To the right can be seen the two-foot high walls that were built to prevent the sea water entering gardens and front doors on occasions such as this.

8. The shore side of the fishermen's cottages situated along the High Street. On this side of the house were situated the kitchens, and the privies which were just holes in the floor through which everything was thrown. This would then be washed away by the tide when it rose. On the far left was one of the barns in which the oysters were packed. Next door is the back of the old pub 'The Anchor Bleu'.

9. Schooners unloading alongside the Quay. The right hand vessel 'Excel' has a rope attached from the top of her mast to a ring on the far side of the Quay. This was regularly done with vessels which were not completely flat-bottomed in order that they should stay upright and lean against the Quay when the tide went out—otherwise the vessel would topple over outwards.

10. Trading vessels lying alongside the Quay. One such vessel was the 'Lady of the Lake' of 84 tons, built by Thomas Smart in 1876, and operated by him bringing coal from Newcastle and sometimes taking away a cargo of corn. He sold her in 1910. She was sunk by enemy action in 1916 off the Start.

11. Sailing boats lying alongside the Quay. In the distance can be seen the little hamlet of 'Gosport'.

COPY OF THE CHARTER OF BOSHAM

JAMES by the Grace of God, of England, Scotland, France, and Ireland, King. Defender of the Faith, etc.

"To All and singular Sheriffs, Mayors, Bailiffs, Constables, Officers and all other loving Subjects, as well within or without our liberties to whom these Presents shall come, Greeting. Whereas according to the Custom of our Realm of England hitherto held and obtained all men and Tenants of the Antient Demesne of the Crown of England have been and ought to be free of Toll, Tollage, Pannage, Murage, Carriage and passage thro' our Realm of England and also according to the aforesaid custom all Men and Tenants of the antient Demesne of the aforesaid Crown have been accustomed from the time whereof the Memory of Man is not to the contrary to be exempt from contributing to the Expences of our Parliament or our Progenitors formerly Kings of England or assembling with the Commons of the said Kingdom; and also according to the said Custom the Men and Tenants of the Manors which are the antient Demesne of our aforesaid Crown, for their Lands and Tenements which are held of the same Manors ought not to be put in Assizes, Juries, or Recognizances unless in those of their own Manor or Court. And as well for that the Manor of BOSHAM with its Appurtenances in the County of Sussex, is of the antient Demesne of our Crown existing as for the Easements Granted by our beloved Sister the LADY ELIZABETH late Queen of England in her Chancery by the Treasurer of the Exchequer Chamber as of her Command then sent."

"We will enjoin and command Ye that all and singular Men and Tenants of the Manor of Bosham aforesaid be permitted to be exempt from Homage or Payment of Tolls, Tollage, Pannage, Murage or other thing for Carriage, Passage of Goods, or any other thing throughout our aforesaid Realm. And also from the expences of Soldiers. And also that the same Men and Tenants of the said Manor shall be exempt from Assizes, Juries and Recognizances without the Court held for the same Manor (unless in it, in which in the said Manor, will or ought to be held one) contrary to the above said Custom unless the Lands or Tenements held of any other Tenure for which according to the form of the Statute of the Common Council of our Realm of England is provided in Juries, or Recognizances ought there to be put. And if the aforesaid Men and Tenants of the Manor of Bosham aforesaid shall upon those occasions or any other be Charged, Rated or Impanelled, that Ye do ease them without delay."

In witness whereof we have caused these our Letters to be made Patent. Witness ourself at Westminster the 10th day of January in the Fourth Year of our Reign over England, France, Ireland, etc., etc., etc.

Signed—

CLAPHAM.

12. The Charter of Bosham. King Harold, in 1066, had owned a Manor at Bosham. When he was killed at the Battle of Hastings, William the Conqueror took over the Manor of Bosham as a royal domain. According to Domesday, he stated that 'all men and tenants of the manors which are the ancient Demesne of our Crown' should have certain privileges. This prerogative has been passed down from father to son through the generations. There are few 'Men of Bosham' left today, and those that there are possess a copy of this Charter. These few men still preserve the right to have free anchorage in Chichester Harbour, although they do not retain some of the other privileges, namely 'not to be put in assizes, juries or recognizances . . . also from the expenses of Soldiers'.

13. One of the gravel barges lying on the hardstanding beside Shore Road. These barges came in laden with gravel at high tide and positioned themselves on the hardstanding. When the tide went out the horse-drawn carts could stand alongside the barges to unload the gravel.

14. The carts belonging to A. H. Edwards, Coal, Coke, Wood, Oil, Gravel and Sand Merchants, loading up at the Quay. Their premises were where the Bosham Service Station now stands.

15. William Coward at the top of his hayrick, hard at work at Church Farm House, Old Park Lane.

16. A Governess cart and Doug, the horse, outside Church Farm House in Old Park Lane.

17. (*right*) Church Farm House in Old Park Lane. There are three farm houses in the parish which bear this name—the farms would have been owned by the Church and let out to tenant farmers.

18. (*below*) The Coward family help drive home the cows at milking time at Church Farm House in Old Park Lane.

19. The thatched barn belonging to Church Farm House which is in Bosham Lane, opposite The Grange (now the Millstream Hotel). The barn has now been demolished to widen the corner opposite the Congregational Church.

20. Edith Coward outside the stables of Church Farm House in Old Park Lane.

21. Farmer and miller, George Brown, watches children at play in front of his Mill on the Quay.

22. The Church and Quay Meadow. The cow grazing and the cart were owned by George Brown, owner of the Mill House, to the left of the picture. He was a staunch Churchwarden and his name appears on the Church Bell that was recast in 1901.

23. Farmer Brown's dairy at the side entrance of his home, Mill House. In recent renovations in this area, remnants of medieval ironworks were found, together with a Roman coin and marble, suggesting that this site must have been occupied for many centuries. The Brook is artificial and may have been constructed by the Romans. After the demolition of the Parsonage House (which had been part of the old Monastery buildings) in 1840, Mill House was occupied by the Vicar until the new Vicarage was built at the northern end of Walton Lane (which used to be called Vicarage Lane) in the mid-19th century.

24. The Mill Pond which was north of the Church. It was fed by the Brook, which runs behind the trees on the left. Mill House is to the right of the Church.

25. A print made in 1893 by Yeend King of the Brook at the point at which, from the bridge alongside, the locals collected their drinking water. The stone in the centre was where everyone stood when dipping their buckets. In the background is the Mill and to the right ships at the Quay.

26. Cut Mill at the northern end of the creek which lies to the west of the village. There were 11 mills operating in the area at the time of Domesday in 1086. There are still the remains of Cut Mill, Broadbridge Mill and Quay Mill, while Racton Mill is still working.

27. Bosham Lane with the Baker's cart outside 'The Gloucester', another of Bosham's many pubs. It is now a private house. On the right side of the road were situated three 'dip holes' from which the locals obtained their water, other than drinking water.

28. The milk float from which the liquid was dispensed by measure into the customers' own jugs, the milkman coming round twice a day with the fresh milk. The little building on the right is the only place in Bosham where one may sometimes get a cup of tea. The barn behind was built in the First World War to house the fire engine. Both are scheduled for demolition in the foreseeable future—that is if they have not fallen down before.

29. Chichester Dairies continue to deliver the milk, even at high tide, to the shipyard. The shed was built in order that the 'Prince of Wales' could be constructed under cover.

30. Mr. Norris, who ran a carrier business, stands on the little bridge that was the beginning of the path to the Portsmouth Turnpike Road at Cutmill. On the right are the two Trevett girls who lived in the Grange, in the garden of which they are standing.

31. The Carrier, Mr. Lemon of the Swan, owned this covered wagon, which took passengers to Chichester daily at a cost of 3d. for the round trip. Jim Ede, Bert Holden, Mr. Trussler and Bill John pose for their picture outside the 'Anchor' in the High Street.

32. The dustcart does his round along Shore Road at high tide.

33. Bosham Lane leading down into the sea. On the left is Richardson's shop which was custom made as a grocer's shop after Mrs. Richardson had come into some money. Their previous shop was along the 'Craut', or High Path. On the right is the entrance to the Manor House.

34. Bosham Lane during one of the very high spring tides in 1935. On the right is Glyn Martin's garage. The tide normally comes no further than Folletts Grocers Shop, the last building on the right hand side.

35. Bosham Lane at Chapel Corner. Behind the pair with the cart is the Congregational Church Hall. To the right are the barns that used to belong to Church Farm House.

36. Mr. Redman and his son at work in the blacksmith's forge in Walton Lane. They were the third and fourth generations of blacksmiths to work in this building and, alas, were the last.

37. A group standing outside the blacksmith's cottage in Walton Lane. Laurel Cottage, which dates back to 1679, was owned by the Cheeseman family of Strange Hall and rented to the Redmans, the blacksmiths.

38. H. Selwyn Lloyd outside the front door of the Manor, which he bought in 1899 and where all his three children were born. He was the author of a book 'A Thumbnail Sketch of Bosham' as well as a number of songs including 'Bosham by the Sea'. He was also a great photographer and took a number of photographs of the village from about 1899 until the First World War. He and his family were great supporters of local activities. He sold the Manor in 1913 and moved into the Grange.

39. H. Selwyn Lloyd with his daughter and a friend outside Gordon Terrace in Bosham Lane in the 1930s.

40. Young Selwyn Lloyd, photographed by his Father, with his Great Aunt Dora, and his mother Caroline in the grounds of the Manor House.

41. Young Selwyn Lloyd, who was born in the Manor House in 1901, being taken for a walk by his nanny Margaret.

42. Mrs. Bryant, the cook, at the back door of the Manor House in 1903.

43. A cheerful pair of maids outside the back door of the Manor House in 1901—photographed by their employer, H. Selwyn Lloyd.

44. Duke the gardener, mowing the lawn of the Manor House in 1903.

45. Mr. and Mrs. Pennett, taken in 1901. They kept house for the Selwyn Lloyd family at the Manor House.

46. H. Selwyn Lloyd photographed by a governess cart in 1902.

47. Dora Lloyd aged 92 in 1901 outside the windows of the Manor House, photographed by her great nephew, H. Selwyn Lloyd.

48. H. Selwyn Lloyd with his wife Caroline and their young son Selwyn with Royal (the dog) outside the front door of the Grange. All three of them are now buried in the Churchyard in Bosham which as a family they loved so much. Young Selwyn died of war wounds in 1949.

49. The Grange in 1913, after it had been purchased by the Selwyn Lloyd family. This building has now been considerably enlarged and is the Millstream Hotel. The brook runs past it at the bottom of the garden. To the right is the Malt House.

50. Chapel Corner with the doorway to the Congregational Church Hall on the left. To the right is the Grange, built in 1770, with the Malt House on the far right. The Grange was bought by H. Selwyn Lloyd in 1913.

51. Strange Hall, the home for many years of the Cheeseman family, holders of the offices of Coroner and Admiral. The family have a vault underneath the Chancel in the Church.

52. Broadbridge House, now demolished, which stood in Delling Lane next door to the farm of the same name. It was owned for many years by the Heaver family. The Heavers were strong supporters of every activity in the village, including regattas and the Women's Institute. The house was occupied by the Home Guard during the Second World War, while there was a factory in the garden making an Austrian type cheese. In the grounds of the Farm was found in 1832 the remains of a Roman Villa and Amphitheatre.

53. The keeper at his duties at the Tollgate across the roadway that runs past the Church. Before the Railway was built through Bosham in 1846 this would have been the road to Portsmouth which ran past the Church and then northwards along the east side of the Cutmill creek to join the Turnpike Road at Cutmill. This is still a public pathway. The old thatched house on the left, which fell down shortly after this photograph was taken, was the school, and Rosie Frogbrook recalled when her grandmother was the school teacher and lived in this building, she took her daughter, Rosie's mother, down into an underground passageway that the young girl was told ran from the Church to the Anchor pub, which is just behind where the photographer would have stood to take this picture. The little girl broke off a small piece of stalagmite which Rosie Frogbrook, who died in her eighties in the 1960s, had in her possession.

54. Duck shooters return home with their booty. Note the little girl with her hoop.

55. Until comparatively recently, all burials of those who died in the village of Chidham had to take place in Bosham. There are records in the Church that show that on several occasions the service was postponed for several days owing to bad weather. Before the dyke was breached which lay between the Apps Shipyard off Quay Meadow and Chidham, bodies could be brought over along the seawall. Before and after the 'dyke' era in the early part of the 19th century, people and coffins were punted across in flat-bottomed boats.

56. Wilfred and Percy Gardener in front of the Mill.

57. This photograph, taken by Dr. Buckle from the top of the Church tower, shows part of the village, the hamlet of Gosport, on the opposite side of the Creek. There was quite a community there with its own little shop and a pub, the latter now a private house called Benbow. Nearly all these buildings have been pulled down, with the exception of Benbow and five cottages, now knocked into one house called Cossick.

58. Brigham Arnold with his bride, a widow, a former Miss Martin, and their guests outside her home in Gordon Terrace. Amongst their guests were Mrs. Holden (to the right of the bride) whose husband ran the Coal Yard behind The Grange, and Jeff Arnold, the young boy on the far left.

59. The first year of the new village school in 1896. The school had moved from the old National School at the top of the creek which had been built in 1837. This building was demolished in 1976 and rebuilt, but the weathervane pictured here has been transferred to the new building.

60. The Post Office and Country Stores in Bosham Lane. In the lower room of the Post Office (the windows of which are on the far left of the photograph) was where the Bosham telephone exchange was placed. The owner of the shop had to do all three jobs at once: serve customers, sell stamps and answer the telephone. The house next door to the Post Office is called 'Riverside'—because, one imagines, the Brook flows past the other side of all these buildings. On the far right is the Congregational Church.

61. The shop window of the Country Stores in Bosham Lane, afterwards re-named 'The Bosham Stores'.

62. The Walton Pub which used to stand halfway down Walton Lane on the East side. It was frequented mostly by the casual labour that came to Bosham during the winter season to help with the oyster fishing. These men slept 'rough' in the fields behind the inn.

63. The War Memorial for those who died in the Great War, 1914-18, was built by a group of local volunteers on the edge of Quay Meadow overlooking the sea, in 1923. The volunteers included Colin Chapman, Harry Grender, Mr. Brierley and his son Bob, George Ede, Jim Ede and Tom New.

64. Their work completed, the craftsmen pose for a photograph. From left to right they are Colin Chapman, Harry Grender, Bob Brierley, George Ede, Tom New and George's brother, Jim Ede. Harry Grender was the local bricklayer.

65. Another photograph of the volunteers. From left to right they are Colin Chapman, Harry Grender, Bob Brierley, George Ede, Tom New and Jim Ede.

66. Two small boys, both of them 'Men of Bosham', Ted and Jack Gilby (on the far left centre of the photograph), together with their sister (in white fur in the foreground) Hilda, were amongst those who joined the procession past the barn of Church Farm House in Bosham Lane on their way to the unveiling of the War Memorial on November 11th 1923.

67. George Ede (with the moustache) amongst the locals marching past the barn of Church Farm House on Armistice Day, 1923.

68. Clifford Scales (the furthest left), the headmaster of the village school, was one of the Choir that joined in the singing for the unveiling of the War Memorial. Two away from him (with the white moustache) was Ernest Layzell who ran one of the local bakeries. The gentleman with the dark moustache to the left of the tree is Harry Follett, who ran the grocer's shop in the High Street.

69. The War Memorial was unveiled by the Rev. Maunder, Vicar of Bosham. Behind is the boathouse of the Apps Shipyard.

70. (*left*) A visit by the late Queen Mary, consort of King George V, in 1923.

71. (*below*) Queen Elizabeth, consort of King George VI, paid a visit to Bosham in 1947, and here is seen talking to the Brownies and Guides. On the left is the Vicar, the Rev. Chatsworth. The Queen was in Court mourning for one of Queen Victoria's grandchildren who had recently died.

72. Another photograph of George VI's Consort at the time of her visit to Bosham in 1947.

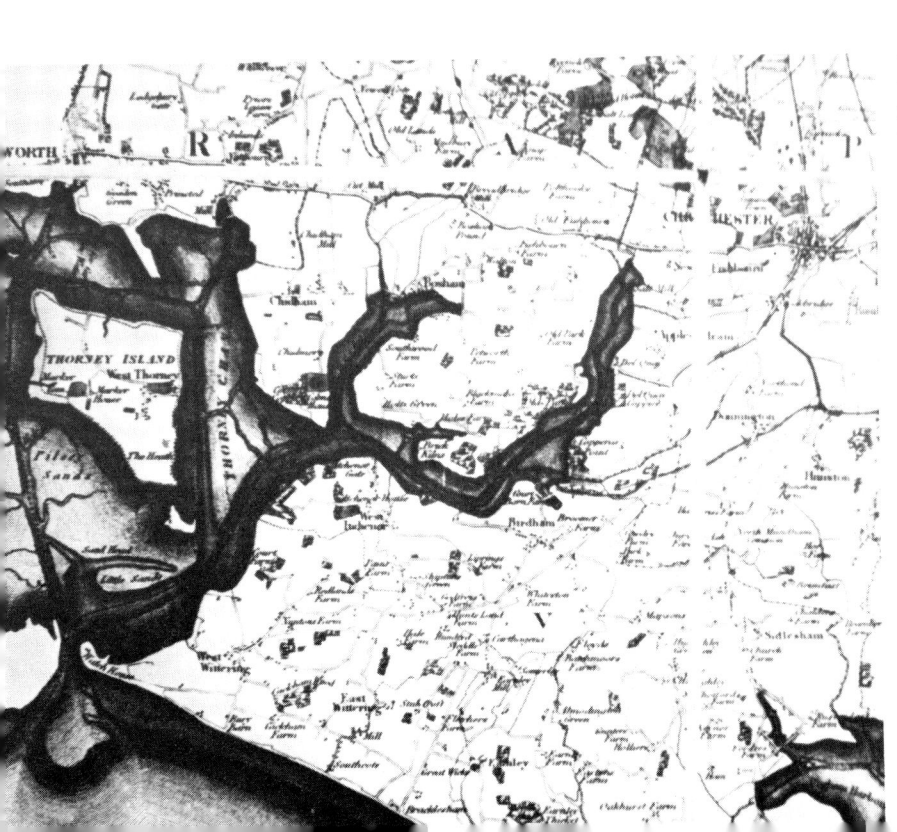

73. A Map of 1825. It shows the land north of Mud Wall, reclaimed, with just a stream running down from Cut Mill. After the gale of 1840, all the land from Mud Wall to Cut Mill was flooded and reverted to being a tidal creek. The oyster fishermen sited their nursery beds in this area.

74. Bosham Village on 4th October, 1936. It shows Mud Wall, a dyke which ran from Chidham (on the right) across to what had been the Apps Shipyard (centre of picture on the shore). This dyke was built at the end of the 18th century and the land north of it, the Cut Mill Creek, reclaimed for farming. In the 1840s a tremendous gale breached the dyke and it has never been restored. This dyke recalls the story of Canute, who is said to have sat on a chair, surrounded by his courtiers, and ordered back the tides—unsuccessfully the chronicles state. It is probable that Canute built a dyke, the Saxon word for which is 'Char', but for some reason the dyke did not hold back the seawater. Mud Wall would be the most likely place for Canute to have built his 'char'.

THE CHURCH

Christianity has probably been preached in Bosham for upwards of two thousand years. Certainly there were preachers of the faith here long before St. Augusta landed in Dover. The church as it stands today is thought to have been built on the site of a Roman Basilica; the bases of the Chancel Arch are all that is left of that earlier building.

The present building is largely Saxon, the first parts of it being built in the early eleventh century during the reign of Canute, a Danish King and the first monarch to unite all England. He is known to have had a Manor at Bosham.

Between the Chancel arches, during renovations in the Church in 1865, a small stone Saxon coffin was found containing the bones of an eight-year-old girl. Tradition had it that a daughter of Canute was drowned in the Brook that runs alongside the Church and had been buried within the building. Also in the Church is a stone effigy of a small girl with her feet on the Royal Lion of England and the Raven of Denmark. This effigy fits the top of the Saxon coffin perfectly but is of a period some two hundred years after Canute. Edward I, who reigned from 1272 to 1307, is known to have visited Bosham in 1286. He was known for his generosity in providing, where none existed, tombs and stone effigies to anyone he felt had not been venerated sufficiently. So it is probable that he ordered the carving of this little stone figure.

The Chancel was built in three stages—the first in the somewhat untidy stonework of the Saxons, followed by the neat herringbone of the Normans and finally the style of the Early English. The east window of the Chancel is one of the finest examples of an Early English window in the Country.

The tower too was built in three stages, Roman bricks being used in the lower section. The Spire was added in the 14th century. There is a little Saxon window at the top of the tower from which may be seen the harbour entrance five miles away. A lookout posted at the window would be able to give the villagers some hours' warning of approaching raiders. When the alarm went up, the entire village would hasten to the Church and the oak doors would be firmly barricaded. Within the Church the very high windows would protect the inmates from the attackers' arrows and stones.

St. Wilfred, visiting Bosham in A.D. 681, found a Celtic Monk named Dicul with six disciples endeavouring to convert the heathen locals to the faith, with little apparent success. There continued to be monks of some sort in Bosham until the Reformation.

The 'College' was situated immediately opposite the Church, of which only a little doorway is left. The Monks used the Chancel as their chapel, while the parishioners worshipped in the Nave with an Altar in front of a screen that cut off the Chancel. Attached to the Chancel were two rooms, now used as a Vestry. Here lived a 'guard'—a monk who watched over the Church possessions.

The monks, one gathers from the chronicles, did not always behave in a manner befitting their calling. They did not hold masses on time and their neglect of the fabric of the Church resulted in the roof falling in. They were unable to afford to put the roof back as it was, so a flat roof was built, the corbels of which are believed to depict the faces of such people as the stone-masons, monks and others of that time. These are still to be seen in the Nave and Chancel. During the renovations of the Church in 1865, the roof was restored to its previous height. Henry VIII had very good grounds for dissolving the monastery.

A number of the pillars in the Nave have graffiti scratched on by returning pilgrims and crusaders, for whom Bosham was the first Church they reached on English soil and where they could thank the Lord for their safe return.

The Bayeux Tapestry, a historical piece of embroidery worked at the time of Queen Matilda, wife of William the Conqueror, shows Bosham Church with the Chancel Arch. It was from Bosham that Harold set out in 1064 to parley with William the Conqueror over who would inherit the throne of England after the death of Edward the Confessor, whose wife was a sister of Harold. As the Manor and Church were owned by Harold who had been crowned King of England, upon his death at the Battle of Hastings in 1066 William took over the estate as a Royal possession. In Domesday Book of 1084, Bosham Church, having been separated from the Manor by William, was one of the wealthiest Churches in England. Unlike most Churches mentioned in Domesday that only possessed a few acres of land, property owned by the Church in Bosham amounted to some thirteen thousand acres in different parts of England, but mostly in the neighbouring parish of Thorney. Henry II declared Bosham Church a Chapel Royal.

75. This scene from the Bayeux Tapestry shows the Chancel Arch of Bosham Church with Harold praying before he left for Normandy in 1064 to discuss with William (afterwards the Conqueror) as to who should inherit the throne of England on the death of Edward the Confessor, Harold's brother-in-law.

76. Bosham Priory. An etching made from one of Grimm's paintings, now in the British Museum. The doorway on the right is very similar in style to a gateway in the wall opposite the south door of the Church.

77. Bosham Parsonage House. The half of the monastery building which was used as the Vicarage after the dissolution of the Order. This building was demolished in the 1840s. The windows on the right are the same as in the previous etching on the left of the building.

78. An engraving done by Nibbs in the 1840s shows the Church with a flat roof, although the marks from a previous higher roof can be seen. There is a story that a donkey was put on the roof to eat the grass that grew. The roof was restored to its original height in 1865.

79. An engraving of Bosham Church. This shows the guard house, the little 'lean-to' in the middle, in which lived a monk who kept watch over the church valuables. From his two windows he could see anyone approaching the Church from the land side. Inside he had one small room downstairs and one upstairs which he approached by a small ladder. He had a kitchen range which kept him warm. On the left at the end of the Chancel can be seen the very beautiful Early English window which was built in 1120.

80. Dr. Buckle the photographer took this picture in 1901 when the Church tower was being repaired. He was an enthusiastic photographer and took many many photographs of Bosham, some of which were made into postcards and sold locally.

81. One of H. Selwyn Lloyd's photographs taken in 1903 of the Church, the Meadow and Brook House.

82. (*left*) This is one of the sketches by Henry Henshall drawn for the Rev. K. H. MacDermott's book 'Bosham Church, its history and antiquities' written in 1911. The buildings, sited behind the Mill House, were used by Farmer Brown.

83. (*below*) The South Aisle of Bosham Church with the Norman Font on the left. On the right, under the window is the entrance to the Crypt, thought to be the site of Dicul's little monastery.

84. In 1903, this bell from the Church was recast. Before it was replaced in its position in the tower, the Churchwarden, Farmer George Brown, had his son christened in the up-turned bell by the Vicar, the Rev. MacDermott. This photograph recalls the legend of the Bosham Bell. Centuries ago, the coast was frequently raided by Danish pirates. When the villagers got warning of the approach of these raiders, they barricaded themselves in the Church. Normally the pirates would ransack the village and leave with their spoils. On this occasion they broke down the door of the Church and, in spite of the entreaties of monks and villagers, stole one of the Church bells and rowed away down the harbour. At 'Bell Pool', off Cobnor Point, the stolen bell fell through the bottom of the pirate's boat and ever since, when the Church bells ring, the stolen bell answers from the deep.

85. The inside of the Parish Church of the Holy Trinity, photographed in about 1900. The Chancel is still the same as that shown in the Bayeux Tapestry. Note the heating boiler on the left—also the paraffin lamps. The Crypt is under the flat stone slab on the right. It is on the pillars on the right of the photograph that graffiti made by returning pilgrims can be seen.

86. (*above*) An etching of Bosham Church Crypt done by Nibbs. This is believed to be the site of Dicul's little monastery that St. Wilfred came upon in A.D. 681. One wonders what the old lady is doing with her faggots. Perhaps they were to feed the heaters upstairs.

87. (*right*) George ('Grandsire') Arnold with his wife outside their cottage in Bosham. Grandsire Arnold joined the village choir in 1829, when he was 10 years of age. He sang in the choir almost until he died at the age of 93 in July 1912. He was the longest practising choirboy in England.

88. (*above*) A picnic party at Kingley Vale in 1914. At all the major church festivities, Christmas, Easter and the Harvest Festival, the girls of the village and anyone else available to join them went up to Kingley Vale, a beautiful forest about three miles north of the village, where they gathered flowers and greenery with which to decorate the church. The next day all the floral decorations were put in the church. It apparently took the whole day and the decorators were given lunch in the upstairs room of the 'Anchor', by the Vicar.

89. (*right*) The Bosham Congregational Church, built in 1837 at a total cost of £500.

FISHING AND SHIPBUILDING

Situated as it is at the top of a creek in the inland waterway that is Chichester Harbour, men must have fished here from the Iron Age once the ability to make dug-out canoes from the vast oak forests that abounded in the area had been realised. Certainly there were mackerel, bass and mullet in abundance, as well as shrimps, oysters, cockles and mussels.

According to a Northumbrian Monk named Bede, who wrote a book 'The Ecclesiastical History of the English Nation', St. Wilfred came to Bosham in 681 A.D. and taught the men of Bosham how to fish. It is thought that St. Wilfred showed the locals, who probably until then had only fished in the shallows with small nets, that by joining the nets together they could go into deeper waters and catch larger fish.

A Saxon Chronicle tells how in the eighth century, when Bosham was one of the leading towns in Sussex, no Lord of the Manor on the shores of Chichester Harbour could get any man to answer the call to arms after the mackerel season had started in August. Mackerel fishing continued on a commercial scale until quite recently.

There was a large oyster industry which, until the limpets attacked the molluscs in 1922, had been second only to Whitstable. A number of medieval walls made of oyster shells have been found during archaeological 'digs' within the village. When the railway came through the village in 1846, it was then possible to get the fish as far as London within a day and thus expand the trade. The oysters were dredged up from the Solent and from as far away as the French Coast in 25 to 30 foot boats, and dropped within the harbour to grow for two or three years. There were as many as 40 boats operating from Bosham. When of a marketable size the oysters were again dredged up and placed in nursery beds, which were situated immediately around the Quay, to clean themselves for at least 15 days. As the orders came in, so the oysters were brought ashore, packed into pannier baskets and taken to the station by donkey. The fishermen formed themselves, with a certain amount of outside financial support, into a Co-operative Society and earned a good wage for those times through the winter months.

In 1665 during the Great Plague, a man came down from London and died of the disease in a Chichester pub. In order to prevent the spread of the plague, the elders of Chichester decided to close the gates of the city and allow no-one to enter or leave. The beleagured townsfolk attached notices to the gates asking anyone to bring them food and leave it at the gates for the townsfolk to collect. The fishermen of Bosham answered the appeal by bringing fish and other food to the City gates every day. In turn the people of Chichester left money for the food in buckets of water—the only form of sterilisation they knew in those days. Thereafter the men of Bosham were permitted to sell their goods in Chichester without payment of Hawkers' Licences. Prior to the present system of Income Tax and County rates, towns raised money locally by demanding licenses of anyone selling goods in the area.

The fishermen lived in the terraces of houses along the shore and in the High Street, for which at the turn of the last century they paid 2s. 6d. a week rent. When yachting became an occupation of the rich in the 1800s, the fishermen crewed during the summer months in such famous yachts as the 'Sir Thomas Lipton', 'Shamrock' and 'Britannia', spending the winter months fishing in Bosham.

The boats for the fishermen must have been built locally. The two creeks were well protected from really heavy seas and strong winds—an admirable situation for shipbuilding.

The first picture that remains to this day of Bosham is in the Bayeux Tapestry in which, in 1064, Harold is shown setting forth with his entourage in longboats—boats that probably would have been built in the area.

Certainly at the end of the nineteenth century, there were at least two boatyards along the shore, both of them building Schooners of up to 500 tons. The older of the two yards, which was situated alongside Quay Meadow, the Apps Shipyard, appears to have built the majority of the larger ones. The other yard, which was sited on the Craut (the Saxon word for right of way) or High Path beyond the Trippet (the Trippet was the name given only to that part of the pathway between the houses behind 'Town Hall'), built most of the fishing boats and was run by the Smart family until sold to Abraham Apps a brother of the older yard's owner. A house called 'The Haven' was subsequently built on the site of this yard.

Further along the High Path at the other end of Mariners Terrace another yard was started by Alex Fowler. He built a large passenger vessel for Littlehampton, 'The Lady Nancy'. This was followed by the 'Prince of Wales'.

It was this Mr. Fowler, who, tired of walking around the top of the Creek past the school to his home on Gosport side for his lunch every day, constructed a Hard across the Creek from the yard to his house which is still there 50 years later. The tin sheds which Alex Fowler built were destroyed by fire in the 1960s.

90. A painting of the Quay sometime in the mid 1850s.

91. This photograph taken from the top of the tower by Dr. Buckle shows the oyster nursery beds into which the oysters were put for a minimum of fifteen days to clean themselves before being packed ready for dispatch. In the foreground can be seen the allotments which were sited on what was then known as Bulls Field, off the High Street immediately opposite the 'Anchor'. At the top of the creek is the Church of England village school which was built in 1837. At high tide it would have been quite a wet walk to school from the village. When this photograph was taken this school would no longer have been used as such for in 1896 a new school was built.

92. The waterfront of Bosham. Beyond the boat can be seen the white roof of one of the barns in which oysters were sorted and packed before shipment to London and other places. It was also used as a butcher's shop once a week.

93. Alan Arnold in his oyster boat off the Quay.

94. Another of H. Selwyn Lloyd's photographs of an oyster boat taken in 1901.

95. Phil Coombes (on left) and Charlie Stoveld (bending down) assist in packing oysters on the Quay.

96. Charlie Stoveld in his dinghy.

97. (*right*) The 'Iona', with her crew in 1898, who included 'Grampy' Gilby (third from left) with another Gilby relative standing behind him.

98. (*below*) Arthur White steadies a boat while his mate continues to shrimp just below the Quay.

99. Ned Coombes, otherwise known as 'Sugar Plum'. He owned one of the biggest oyster boats in the harbour.

100. The largest fishing boat in the Bosham fleet, being some thirty feet long. It was owned by Ned Coombes. This lino cut was used for many years on the cover of the Parish Magazine.

101. A fisherman scrubs the bottom of his boat in front of Quay Cottage.

102. Bill and Jack Arnold loading their nets at the Quay in 1902.

103. The vessel 'Thetis' alongside the Quay in Bosham in 1901. She was owned by George Martin, a brother of the owners of the pubs 'The Anchor' and 'The Ship'.

104. One of H. Selwyn Lloyd's photographs taken in 1901 at the end of the Quay.

105. A trading vessel alongside the Quay. Beyond is the raptackle, one of the barns in which oysters were packed. Although the building bears the name 'raptackle', which implies that rope was made there at some time, there is no history of this industry and the building is not long enough for such a job. It is possible that rope was made on the Quay while the 'raptackle' housed the tools for the trade.

106. A schooner at low tide on the mud just off Shore Road.

107. (*above*) The Schooner 'Nugget' alongside the Quay in 1902. Her port of registry was Arundel and she is listed in the first Mercantile Navy List of 1857. She was bought by Thomas Smart, the owner of the second shipyard along the High Path in 1878.

108. (*left*) The 'Emerald' being unloaded alongside the Quay.

109. (*above*) The yacht 'May' preparing to set sail from Bosham in about 1903 with her crew of Bosham fishermen.

110. (*right*) One of H. Selwyn Lloyd's photographs of the beginning of a sailing trip from Bosham.

111. The yachts line up along the Quay while the crew, mostly of Bosham oystermen, prepare to stock ship for the summer yachting season.

112. Some of the dinghies (tenders) from the yachts lined up under the Quay. A small portable jetty enabled the yachtsmen and their wives to climb into the dinghies dryshod.

113. The slipway of the Apps shipyard alongside Quay Meadow.

114. A sketch done by Stanley Cook in 1888. It is of the Apps Shipyard which was sited just off Quay Meadow to the west of the Church. The vessel under construction is thought to be the 'Good Hope' which was on the stocks for some twenty years.

115. (*above*) The 'Good Hope' almost ready for launching on the stocks of the Apps Shipyard. She was launched on 14 July 1904 and started her first voyage on 3 May 1905. Behind the vessel can be seen the shed of the Apps Shipyard, while under the tree is the blacksmith's shop. Both buildings still stand today.

116. (*left*) Thomas Apps, the owner of the shipyard alongside Quay Meadow.

117. The 'Good Hope' under sail from a painting owned by Thomas Apps' grand-daughter Mrs. Bevan, née Hickman.

118. Two small girls play in front of the Apps Shipyard building. To the left is the covered shed where the smaller boats were built.

119. The Apps Shipyard was purchased by Lord Iveagh in the 1920s and leased to Spencer and Brice, who continued to operate it as a small shipyard.

120. The village taken from a position near the old village school built in 1837. Along the path on the right the village children had to walk but in those far off days it was not as it is seen in this photograph. The stream had to be crossed. In order that the schoolgirls should not get their long dresses wet, the boys had to bring the school forms and put them over the stream, thus enabling the girls to arrive dryshod. The large buildings on the right were built in order that the 'Prince of Wales' be constructed under cover.

121. The 'Prince of Wales' was the largest flat-bottomed passenger vessel built in the world and was launched in 1923. From the stories of the launching party it was a very jolly affair. Builders and owners had consumed a great deal by the time the tide was high enough to launch her. She went down the launching pad with such verve that she shot across the channel and grounded on the other bank. As there was only one tide high enough to launch her, a great deal of hard work had to be done very quickly to get her off the mud again and down the channel. She was built for Southend Navigation Company who operated her on the Thames. She was 108 feet long.

122. The vessel 'Dolly Varden' being built at the Smart yard on the High Path. The break in the wall can be seen. There was a bridge across the pathway at this point which was lifted when a ship was ready for launching.

123. Gregory Major, one of the local seamen, with his parrot in the High Street. On the right are two little cottages. 'Bosham Castle' used to be the barber's establishment before the First World War. The story is told of one very nervous young man who, during the course of a train journey from London to Bosham in the 1930s, disclosed to a fellow traveller that he had been invited down by a young lady to stay with her parents in 'Bosham Castle'. He was much concerned as to whether he had brought the correct wearing apparel for what he imagined to be one of Britain's stately homes. The fellow traveller was loathe to divulge to him that 'Bosham Castle' consisted of four tiny rooms, two up and two down! The house at the end of the row is the Town Hall.

124. Gregory 'Grandpa' Major mends his nets on the steps of his home on Shore Road.

125. A more formal portrait of Mr. and Mrs. Gregory Major.

126. Mr. and Mrs. Charlie Hickman. He was the blacksmith at the Apps shipyard alongside Quay Meadow and married his boss's daughter, Edith Apps.

127. The small girl who was to become Mrs. Bevan was the daughter of Charlie Hickman and his wife.

128. (*right*) Another photograph of Edith Hickman.

129. (*below*) The 'Anchor' and, two doors away, 'The Ship' which at the time this photograph was taken were owned by the two Martin brothers.

FAIRS, FETES AND REGATTAS

One forgets today, as one sits watching the television or listening to the radio, that fifty years ago entertainment had to be self-produced. So such things as fairs, fetes and regattas which occurred regularly in the village on specified days of the year, were much planned and were something to which everyone looked forward.

Fairs have obviously been part of the Bosham scene for many centuries for in 1081 Roger de Montgomery, Earl of Arundel, the owner of the Manor of Bosham, was given permission to hold six yearly fairs in the village. Fairs continued to be held in the village until the 1950s. On 20 May every year the Fair for the school treat was held on 'Fairfield', (there is a house and a road which still bear the name) when the children from the school enjoyed all the amusement free until a certain time of the day, funds being provided by local benefactors. Another fair was held on the day of the Regatta on Quay Meadow, and on Bull's Field, the area north of the High Street, adjacent to the Churchyard. Some of the stalls would be set up in the High Street. There would be boxing booths, hoop-la, coconut shies and other such things. In fact, there are many local families who now own a pair of china dogs (which fetch large sums of money in antique shops) won or bought for a few pence by their grand-parents and great-grandparents at these fairs.

Then there were the Fetes—these went on for two or three days from two in the afternoon to ten at night. The railways ran special excursions from Brighton and Portsmouth. The Band of the Royal Sussex Regiment played, that is when such things as Maypole dancing, the Morris dancers or the Humorous Concert were not taking place.

Another great event was the Annual Regatta, held under the distinguished patronage of such V.I.P.'s as His Grace the Duke of Richmond and Gordon K.G., The Right Honourable Lord Gifford V.C. and the Lord Bishop of Chichester. Before the formation of the Bosham Sailing Club, the various fishing fleets (Emsworth, Itchenor and Bosham) in the harbour used to compete against each other. When the present Bosham Sailing Club was formed in 1921 races were still run for fishermen in Chichester Harbour as well as for the various classes of Bosham's fishing fleet. In the far off days of 1908 there was a Handicap Motor-Boat race for which there were only three entries and the first prize was 21 shillings. There was also a double-handed Rowing Race in Bosham fishing boats for ladies, the prizes for which included an umbrella, a lady's skirt, a lady's handbag and 2lb. of tea. The Committee of the Club had to approve the bathing costumes worn for the Long Dive, i.e. the longest distance under water. During the afternoon the Blue Hungarian Band played such things as 'The Bohemian Girl', 'Miss Hook of Holland' and Verdi's 'Travatore'.

There was a male choir that met regularly in the 'Gloucester', and there were 'The Bosham Bonfires', who were also a group of singers. Obviously Boshamites enjoyed their 'Local' for there were no less than eight or nine pubs within a two mile radius of the Church. There was also an acting group. Dinners were frequently held in the upstairs rooms of 'The Anchor' and the 'Gloucester'. Every year there would be an enormous bonfire at Street End on November 5th. People would dress up and sometimes process to join up with other parties from Fishbourne and Chichester.

It was from this necessity to entertain themselves that so many stories and traditions have come down through the generations. What else was there to do during the long evenings, except to listen to Grandad recounting what he had heard from his grandparents? Few could read and fewer still could afford a newspaper.

130. Bosham Manor House decorated for the coronation of Edward VII in 1902.

131. (*left*) Programme for the Swiss Fete in 1904.

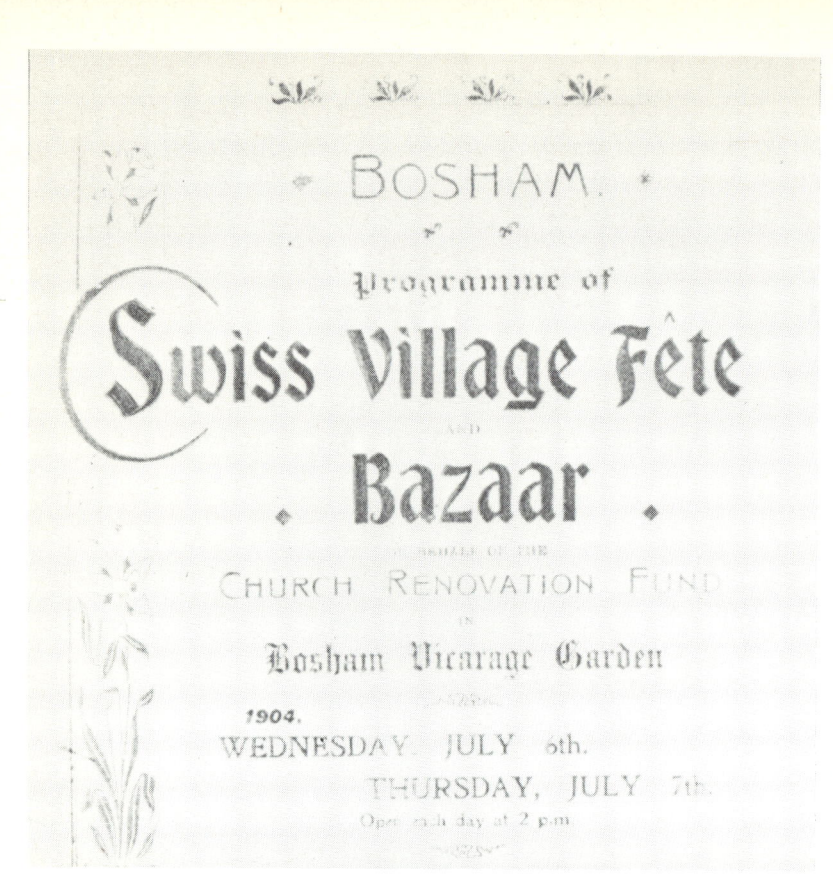

132. (*below*) The Dutch Fete of 1907 which was held in the garden of the Vicarage, now known as Walton House. A large part of the garden must have been where now is situated the Oakcroft Nurseries.

133. (*right*) Miss Heaver dressed up for her part in the Dutch Fete.

134. (*below*) H. Selwyn Lloyd dressed as a Dutchman with the small son of the Vicar, Rev. MacDermott, at the 1907 Fete.

135. (*above*) A panorama of the Dutch Fete from a Vicarage window.

136. (*left*) Caroline Lloyd, her son Selwyn and husband, Hugh, participating in the Fete of 1907.

137. Dressed for the part—Hugh Selwyn Lloyd and 'Lanky' Williams at the Dutch Fete.

138. These fetes were all organised by the very lively Vicar, the Rev. MacDermott. In the group are Roley Heaver (standing second from left) and Maude Heaver (sitting second from right). The Heaver family played a great part in all these Regattas. The family lived at Broadbridge House, which has since been demolished.

139. The Old English Village Fete and Bazaar held in the Vicarage garden on Wednesday and Thursday 3 and 4 July 1912. Amongst those who had 'Refreshments for ye hungrie traveller' were Mrs. Follett (sitting left) and Dolly Follett (far right) whose family ran the grocer's shop at Street End. Next to Dolly Follett is Elsie Smart whose father ran the shipyard on the High Path.

140. The Manor House party enjoying their cup of tea while watching the regatta in about 1901 or 1902. Mrs. Selwyn Lloyd (furthest left of the ladies) has a particularly dashing hat to wear for such an occasion.

141. The Manorial party on board 'Nellie' watching the regatta of 1902. In the middle is young Selwyn Lloyd with his nanny Margaret on the left. The seaman is Uncle Joe.

142. The Regatta of 1902 or 1903 with the fishing boats competing and a yacht dressed overall on the Chidham side.

143. (*left*) The official programme of the Regatta held in 1908.

144. (*below*) The Bosham Regatta of 1910. Dolly Woods, whose father owned the shipyard along the High Path, is the girl to the left of Barbara Brierley in the big hat.

145. The spectators in the Regatta of about 1910 or 1912. They included young Dolly Woods (far right in the vessel). Her mother (six away to the left) was the daughter of Thomas Smart, owner of the Shipyard along the High Path.

146. The greasy pole competition at the regatta of 1913.

147. A scene from one of the sailing regattas of the early 1920s.

148. The poster displayed around the village for the regatta of 1926.

149. Some of the Bosham Fishing Boats taking part in the annual regatta at about the turn of the century.

150. A view during one of Bosham's many regattas. On the Chidham side of the harbour can be seen the wreck of a once-beautiful yacht.

151. More spectators watching the regatta shortly before the first World War.

152. The Committee boat anchored off the Quay for the start of a rowing race during a regatta.

153. The Admiral of Bosham's Coxwain and Crew at a regatta. The title of Admiral of Bosham no longer exists.

154. Chris Moore, one of the local colourful characters, causing amusement at a regatta at the beginning of this century.

155. This is a pageant that was organised for either the Jubilee of George V in 1935, or the Coronation of George VI in 1937. A hayrick was obtained and the participators dressed up in the clothing of a hundred years earlier.

156. The fair on Quay Meadow on Regatta Day in the early 1900s.